Praise for To Phrase a Prayer for Peace

"What is prayer for? It's easy to deride "praying for peace" as a quixotic absurdity in the face of the empire and its industry of mass violence. But Donna Spruijt-Metz's diary poems *To Phrase a Prayer for Peace* are a frank dialogue with the Psalms during the ongoing Gaza conflagration, engaging in that ancient practice of calling out to the divine, and calling out the divine, in a time of divine silence, to ask for an end to this violence, to imagine a path forward. 'I ask YOU,' she writes, 'come close.' That YOU, of course, is not just God, but all of us. 'Witness,' she writes, 'speak light.' We need more poems like this, with their unhardened hearts, in this awful dark."
— Philip Metres, author of *Fugitive/Refuge*

"Aching for Jerusalem from his corner of medieval Spain, the poet and Jewish philosopher Yehuda Halevi famously lamented, 'My heart is in the East, and I in the uttermost West.' In this elegant and moving poetry journal, Donna Spruijt-Metz chronicles her daily life on the West Coast as she follows—with acute distress—Hamas' October 7th attack and the ensuing Israel-Hamas war that has turned the Middle East into a 'lethal puzzle.' Subtle, delicate, and capable of balancing paradoxes, Spruijt-Metz's voice holds a striking contemporary freshness even as David's ancient Psalms serve as her point of departure and time and again, she appeals to the Divine to save the world from the sorrows of war."
— Yehoshua November, author of *The Concealment of Endless Light*

"*To Phrase a Prayer for Peace* is exactly the kind of book I wish to see in the world amid these dark and divisive days, and Donna Spruijt-Metz—with her blazing clarity and generosity of spirit—is just the right person to write it. As a reader, I trust the craft, humor and humility of these poems, perhaps, in part, because they do not claim any easy answers. '[B]ut what do I know / of darkness?' Spruijt-Metz writes, 'My version of darkness / is full of candlelight—'. Arriving on the page seemingly despite themselves ('And now/can I stop / with this?'), and often leveled at an almighty 'YOU,' the poems that shape this timely collection plead and petition, protest and pray. Donna Spruijt-Metz has the strength of heart to envision a better path forward and the poetic chops to share it with us all. "
— Jared Harél, author of *Let Our Bodies Change the Subject*

"From the very first poem, the speaker of *To Phrase a Prayer for Peace* is conflicted: 'even in snow—hoof / paused over the water—my heart says / trust—my tracks say / doubt.' First, her subject is prayer: 'I stand continually before YOU— / but I'm not listening   I am dangerous   I am /   not ready.' Once the war begins, the poems become a record of her internal divisions engaging with it ('what can I do / but watch / look away, watch, look away'), thinking about it ('We both / need a homeland. / Split or share? What / would Solomon do?'), and writing and praying about it. How extraordinary to achieve such honesty, such poignance about so fraught a subject even as it is unfolding. Every page answers her 'need' for 'a poem driven / by the unbearable /dailiness of this / time', a 'time' still ongoing, in which we must still contend with 'the dust and the rubble there / where so many children sleep— / each part of their bodies / hungry—"
    —Jacqueline Osherow, author of *Divine Ratios: Poems*

"*To Phrase a Prayer for Peace* is incantatory and intricate, haunting and lovely. As the days and devastation accumulate the poems do, too; they gather spiritual strength and culminate as an extended hymn. Donna Spruijt-Metz's voice is distinct and resonant. This work is personal. It required her whole self, the sum of her considerable wisdom and lived experience. In order to meet this solemn moment, Spruijt-Metz offers everything she has—abundantly, carefully, and well."
    —Michael Kleber-Diggs, author of *Worldly Things*

"I have long come to Donna Spruijt-Metz's work for comfort, and *To Phrase a Prayer for Peace* left me refusing to leave the embrace of its tender, difficult, and necessary poems. In conversation with the timelessness of Psalms and the ever-timely 'Israel-Hamas War,' she contends with the unanswerable amid atrocity, 'listening—straining in YOUR silence.' The poems in this collection address a 'YOU' who is higher power; a 'you' who is an intimate other; and a 'you' who is all of us, holding these words on our tongues. Language is grounded in the body, in the sensory experience that unites us as humans, as it is in the spiritual world beyond the flesh. In confessing, 'I can't find the courage / tonight / to love,' Spruijt-Metz asks us all to love a little harder, and to find—to create—the light in the darkness because 'My version of darkness / is full of candlelight—'.
    —Julia Kolchinsky, author of *40 WEEKS*

To Phrase a Prayer for Peace

Donna Spruijt-Metz

Wildhouse Poetry

Copyright © 2025 Donna Spruijt-Metz

Design by Melody Stanford Martin

The drawings included in this book are by Gershom Spruijt

Published by Wildhouse Poetry, an imprint of Wildhouse Publishing (www.wildhousepublishing.com). No part of this book may be reproduced in any manner without written permission from the publisher, except in brief quotations embodied in critical articles or reviews. Contact info@wildhousepublishing.com for all requests.

Printed in the USA

All Rights Reserved

ISBN 978-1-961741-20-1

אני ישנה ולבי ער קול

I was asleep, but my heart was awake.

—*Song of Songs 5:2*

Contents

Prelude—Before the Again—
Hoof **5**
To Praise the New **6**
A Prayer for the Ability to Pray **7**
Backbone **8**
Shift **9**
River of Dream **10**

Number Our Days—Again—
Darkness Myth for Day 1 of the Israel-Hamas War—Before I Heard the News **12**
Day 2 of the War **13**
Day 3 of the War: Unknown **14**
Day 4 of the War **15**
Day 6 of the War: Homeland **16**
Day 10—A Broken Eintou **17**
Day 14—Little Power **18**
Day 17—She Asks Me **19**
Fragment for Day 20 of the War **20**
Day 22—Blood Moon **21**
Day 24— **22**
Day 25—And I Am Losing My Grip **23**
Day 26—I am Trying to Focus on the Power of Words— **24**
Day 27—And I would like to stop writing this now **25**
Day 28—Complete Encirclement **26**
Day 31—Speak **27**
On Day 34 of the War I Ask YOU to Teach Us Again **28**
Love Poem for Day 39 **29**
Psalm for Day 42 of the War **30**
Day 45—Water Guilt **31**
Day 46—Another Slog **32**
Thanksgiving Day, Day 48 **33**
On Day 51 of the War, We Go on a Date **34**
On Day 55—An extension **35**

On Day 56—I wake from a dream **36**
On Day 57—Is it a 'Big War' Yet? **37**
On Day 58—I Get Out the Pen and Face the Beast Again **38**
Day 60—I Thought This Would Be a Milestone **39**
Day 61 **40**
Day 63 of the War **41**
Day 64—Word(')s Damage **42**
Psalm for Day 69 **43**
Day 72—Every Deity Will Cry **44**
Day 75—I Step Away to Lick Wounds **45**
Psalm for Day 76 **46**
Day 78, and the news hangs in the air like an overripe fig— **47**
Day 80—And I Know Less Every Day **48**
Day 82—I Want **49**
Psalm for Day 83 **50**
On Day 84—It's between witchcraft and reading the news **52**
It's Day 86 and NO **54**
Psalm for Day 90 **55**
Here's What You Need to Know 93 Days into the War **56**
Day 95—My Friend Summarizes My Days **57**
Day 100 and I Draw Another Line **58**
Day 104—Can YOU Open Me Up **59**
Day 107 of War in the Holy Lands: Heart Wants **60**
Day 110? 111? I Looked Away for a Moment **61**
Day 118—The Proper Way to Phrase a Prayer for Peace **63**

Postlude—It isn't over—
Swarm **67**
Leap Day **68**
Sin-Mouths **69**
Locksmith **70**
Warm Evening, Restless **71**
Crow Comes Back **72**

Notes **75**
Acknowledgments **77**
About the Author **81**
About the Artist **83**

Prelude

—BEFORE THE AGAIN—

Hoof
—after Psalm 89 lines 26-35

Is it that I have had a richness
of choices, have I gazelled
sideways from one riverstone to the next?

    Or has this been a series
    of false starts—
    the hoof withdrawn
    at the slightest snow?

    January's Wolf Moon calls her pups
    into the night—marks
their necessary kill. We all
need to eat

even in snow—hoof paused
over the water—my heart says
trust—my tracks say
doubt

To Praise the New
—after Psalm 111

Delight rushes by—I strain
toward the brass ring—

YOU, the chariot—YOU, the ring—stuttering
in and out of range

& YOU, memory—YOU
are an entire palace—while

for us—nothing holds still—everything
turns new as we try to praise it

—we need to deepen
our generosities—

—what
had I imagined?

time
is not at all—

A Prayer for the Ability to Pray
—after Psalm 109 verses 11-16

I broke   my left hip the first time our daughter left home
it was decades ago   one pain camouflaged   the other
     even though I'm standing   at the threshold

of YOUR cathedral   I can't navigate   my own cargo   how is it
that I always think   tomorrow will finally be
     rain-slicked and fresh

everything gliding out   from under me—mud under bad shoes
As if I am not   broken   at the thought of her   leaving again—
     I turn away   focus on the other pains—the ones of the body

I am before YOU continually—but not listening—not seeing, not lifting,
practicing   some kind of mercy   rehearsing for my own reckoning
     geography and time—miserable constructs   And now I have

fractured my right hip on the eve of her next departure my own kind
of God wrestling   And so she will go   I only have
     two hips to give.   I stand continually before YOU—

     but I'm not listening   I am dangerous   I am
                                not   ready
                                    My Lord

Backbone
               —after *Ps*alm 101, lines 6-8

bat-shaped
       cloud, crescent moon—

              (—our detachments   from YOUR land)

            our lies   YOUR eyes   how we avert,

                 how we life   and ligament

                        fabricate   —we sinew,

                                 we backbone

                   —meanwhile, the planet

                 —oh timepiece, ticky thing,

          timesquanderer.

       We are running out

      And then Morning—that chancy

angel—comes

Shift
          —*after Psalm 104*

Once, YOU positioned the water
over the earth.

     Now, our own hands
fashion the boundaries—frail
and briefly reverent—and then we
forget our place in things, we think
we have become the shifters. But no—

it is the waters that retreat from us—
parched, dry mouthed—our hands
weeping—
Until the waters flood us.

That, too, happens.

We dust off
our divining rods, deploy
submersibles. We want to know
what the waters hold.

We think we want to know
YOUR mind. Don't

look at me like that.

River of Dream
>*—after Psalm 148, verses 1-6*

Here, in this valley
with YOU

(& you & you & you)

      trees listening—intent
      on the voices
      of water & birds—

who
is speaking to whom?

flurry of small stars   —

—a swirling conversation—

No.   I ask YOU—come close—wade
through YOUR heavy waters—
come to me dripping & blessed
come to me shivering—
but come.

Number Our Days

—AGAIN—

Darkness Myth for Day 1 of the Israel-Hamas War— Before I Heard the News
—for R.

I'm a night writer—and no matter how hard I try
to bend myself into daylight
I long for the dark

but what do I know
of darkness? My version of darkness
is full of candlelight—

Day 2 of the War

It is 9:40 pm PST, October 8, 2023.
I have lived
through this day—
through preposterous beauty-dome
of sky, empty
except for all that blue,

—meanwhile, war—
now more.

What can I do
but watch
look away, watch, look away.

Day 3 of the War: Unknown

Monday, October 9th, 2023
7:37 PM—
I am still alive—
but terrified—

my daughter
has gone militant.
But death

is everywhere, and I am not
militant. I am
heartbroken—walking the dogs

tonight, I met a woman. She saw
my Mogen David and needed
to talk. We sobbed
into one another's
unknown.

Day 4 of the War
          #WeAreToast
                —Dana Levin

It is 7:57 pm PST, October 10th, 2023
and I have lived through this day—
I weep from room to room—

It is taught that prayers
said in community
are multicolored—while
individual prayers are monochrome.

We tinker—we are
haphazard technicians—
God is what we need, and fast."*
All Gods welcome.

                *from Adélia Prado

Day 6 of War—Homeland

It's night.
At last, darkness—
at last, room
for my heart.

No more death, I beg.
Palestine
needs water. Jews
need a homeland—

We both
need a homeland.
Split or share? What
would Solomon do?

Day 10—A Broken Eintou

I'll try
to stop counting
the days—maybe I'll opt
for counting weeks—
is that practical or just sad?
Poet friends are writing
in forms—as if
structure

could hold
this grief—as if
structure could clutch the world—
It's already
day 10.

Day 14—Little Power

Hello, silent one.
Are my war poems
making you
uncomfortable?

It's only anguish.

My power
is of the small variety—
the power
of a knock-off crystal—yet
I can't stop them.

The sun, tempered
today by breeze—me
fed and free
in a country where
others are not—

My child
not gone
to war.
And the war
hasn't come to her
—not yet—

but oh my Lord
all the children—
all of them.
All Of Them.

Day 17—She Asks Me

How do you feel
about chestnuts

in mid-autumn
mooncakes?

I tell her
I feel great about chestnuts—

their delicate flavor
in this season of war.

Fragment for Day 20
       —after Psalm 116 verses 1-4

And I am calling out to YOU in this darkness—yet don't know what to say

And I am mounted like an insect in the narrows of judgment

And I'm a coward in the straits of strife—

And I'm asking to imagine a path—

And I am listening—straining in YOUR silence

Day 22—Blood Moon

Tonight, the Hunter's Moon balloons
I am too stomach-sick and world-tired
to fully ritual—but nonetheless,

I set new water out for consecration
under this full moon—I don't
cast a circle or call the spirits down—

the setting out of two blue glass jars
—filled with filtered water—
will need to be enough.

In one, a teaspoon of sea salt I keep
blessed and ready—
in the other, no salt.

Salt water for cleansing —sweet water
for summoning. I am too tired
for an incantation—I add a silver coin,

pass my hand over the jars—and
set them in the moonlight.
Let the waters be hungry—

let them soak up the power—
and that is how it seems tonight,
in this world—

all of us, hunting, bloodthirsty,
blind to the damage our words do
—the untidy rending of friendships and families

Not yet a world at war, no—but look.
Truly look—and see—
let the Blood Moon seep in.

Day 24—

I am sick again,
but this time I understand it better,
the gut's rebellion—

this time I return to the bland

and yes, I am feeling extinct
in this slaughtering season—

my daughter says I don't do well with upheaval—
says I am not great at death and destruction.

It's a weakness.

Day 25—And I Am Losing My Grip

I say something unkind to a stranger.
—and what good does that do?
I just hurt my own soul with this anger—
it bounces, ricochets,
is impotent. Buber praises
those who can dwell
in the "Kingdom of Holy Insecurity"—
rather like Keats' "Negative Capability"—
(or at least akin to it).
Dear friend, I have nothing tonight,
just words. Thoughts. Fears. A poet asks
"Do you think the seas are angry—or
is it the fish?" Everything is wrong with that question.
We humans destroy everything we touch.
And we touch everything. Sticky-fingered
and greedy.

Day 26—I am trying to focus on the power of words—

at the luncheon we hear
students yelling at each other
in the quad—I sit as close
as I can to an exit door—although I would need
to be able to sprint all the way across campus
to reach the safety of my car.
It's about the order of things.
Getting out before they come for me, for instance—
or the order of words.
Are we too late?   transposes into
We are too late—

Day 27 and I would like to stop writing this now

but in our Yiddish poetry class
      —which begins at 4:00 pm—only
      one hour before one can reasonably
      make a cocktail—
we read Aaron Zeitlin.

Zeitlin survived World War II
survived his wife and child—
such strange sentence construction
what is it "to survive?"—

I survived my father
but didn't properly survive
his death—Zeitlin laments
he cannot even lose his mind.

As a teenager, my first therapist
told me that insanity
would not be my way out—that it was
in my genes, perhaps

but not in my makeup—
and I felt trapped inside myself—as we are
now—trapped inside this.
It is day 27
and what is holy?

Day 28—Complete Encirclement

In 2010, the rabbi wandered
through the stone yard
—past patterned granite, marble
veined with greys and amber—

lost in the narrow aisles,
his shoes dulled and dusty—he was seeking
a synagogue

in every stone. Instead
he saw majestic hotels
sleek bathrooms. Forgotten

at the very back of the yard
he found blackened bricks—seared
and uneven—left too long

or fired too high
in their kiln.
He chose these to build

a new synagogue
in the heart
of Amsterdam.

He knew what it meant to be burned.

And now, everything is burning
—how dangerous we have become—

Day 31—Speak

And now
can I stop
with this?

Even though
breath
has become
a privilege?

In the margins
of my innocence
I scribble:
"Let there be peace"

No stopping yet,
girl, old girl,
woman, cowering—

speak. You only have
everything
to lose.

On Day 34 I Ask YOU to
Teach Us Again
    —after Psalm 116 verse 5-8

Ancient concepts:

Nurture
Compassion
Justice

Teach us again.

We are perpetrators
of the unforgivable:

we forget.

Yet even standing
in this rubble
YOU invite us

to return
to peace—
YOU say

return.
YOU
say *tears*.

YOU say
stumble.

And we do.
We stumble.

Love Poem for Day 39

What I want tonight
is only a small thing—

I want to write
that poem about "enough"—
the one that says
"enough of the brutal"—

or the one that starts with "You,
selling roses"—

or to lie
on a white damask
Victorian couch,
my hair coiffed
elaborately, my ardent
breasts draped
in an amber
satin dress—one elegant
hand thrown
across my brow,
a shoe having just fallen
from my delicate foot.

But I don't have
delicate feet, and those poems
have already been written
and I can't find the courage
tonight
to love.

Psalm for Day 42
        —after Psalm 116 verses 9-14

The poet tells us this: once YOU
took two heaps of letters, threw them
from a mountaintop, and scattered them
across all the paths of the world.

We are still trying to puzzle them
into words—the words YOU
surely intended.
Didn't YOU?

We just need a little grace
down here, right now. Maybe
a hint or two on how
to solve
this lethal puzzle—

How can I stand
and be counted—when it is
the counting itself—the sifting
into categories—the willful separation—
that will kill us all?

Day 45—Water Guilt

Last night, I ran
the water
long enough
for it to warm up
before I washed
my face—
a privilege I don't
usually allow myself—

and the guilt came—
reliably—first
California drought
guilt—then desert water
guilt—then planet
water guilt—and now
war water guilt—
the dust-caked faces
of the waterless

Day 46—Another Slog

My husband is wretched
from the new COVID booster

I'm wretched from
too little sleep—

we slog through the evening
until we can go to bed

but we are transfixed
by the news
as it leaks out

perhaps hostages
on both sides
will go free

perhaps they, too
will be able to slog
towards a bed

Thanksgiving Day, Day 48

and we don't celebrate—

instead, we hold our breaths
clock ticking until
it's a reasonable time
for a cocktail—ticking

across the expanse
of another unreasonable
day—we wait
for the release—

On Day 51 of the War, We Go on a Date

17 hostages traded for 39 prisoners—
we trade a few hours of war-worry
for an escape to a
Flamenco concert—

At first, I can't settle into the music.
All I can think about is war
and the full November moon.
But then the pianist
riffs into brilliant fusion—

unspooling me into the red
threads of my childhood
—the jazz hours spent
under my mother's piano—*there's no such thing
as love*—I slip away from this
war—backwards
into a different kind
of war—hello, mom.
It's been a while.

On Day 55—An extension

of cease-fire is possible—and I dream
of a woman in thick braids—I touch
her braids, thick like my own

—we sit on suitcases in an
airport—surrounded
by boxes—one holds a child's

porcelain tea set, and the box is ruined—held together
with rubber bands and tape. We are fleeing,
braids secured

with string— we are
haphazard jigsaws
— string, tape, rubber bands

On Day 56 I wake from a dream

where I am being stifled
by mimeographs &
carbon copies—
like the ones
from my mother's typewriter—

copies of changed passwords
closed bank accounts
—facts, she thought
—but in fact,
they were slippery & intangible
yet set in ink—which makes them

seem true—just like the news

—I wake up—
the nightmare of war
has resumed—

On Day 57—Is it a 'Big War' Yet?

There's a thrumming between my thighs—not
that familiar sex-thrum—no—it's mother-fear
—as if life could still begin there—but yes
a huge wanting—so deep—for this world
to hold my daughter—hold her safe—

a fear, speaking
from inside itself—a fear
of speaking—we kill
as we are killed—how
is this a reflection
of YOU?

Would YOU answer
my womb's roar?
(as if YOU could continue
to love any
of us).

On Day 58 I Get Out the Pen and Face the Beast Again

I'm re-reading Exodus—trying
to understand—who's heart is it

that are YOU hardening now?
So many hard hearts.

Hard: Old English *heard*
"solid and firm, not soft,"

but my mind goes to *hearden*—
and from there: *make unhearing*—to teach

not to listen. The heart, made opaque
& deaf. I am empathy rubbeling

—breaking into bits
of my own stone.

Day 60—I Thought This Would Be a Milestone

The gematria of the Hebrew letter Samech=60.
Beautiful letter ס isn't it? Circular almost, like
the endless cycle of life. A symbol
of support and protection—
completeness.

Was I wrong to think
that day on 60,
beasts of all stripes
would look up
from their prey—teeth
bloodied—
and seek
respite? But no,

It was just another
atrocity day.

Day 61

I have lost track, skipped
days—from this remove
that turns out to be
possible

& unforgivable

Day 63

I walk
through my unbombed neighborhood—
I sit in my white
studio to write to YOU—

and last night I dreamt—
dreams, not nightmares—which means
I fell into some form

of actual sleep—not the exhausted kind,
not the imprisoned kind—not
shelterless.

Do YOU
want to know my dreams, deity?
But don't YOU

already know?

Day 64—Word(')s Damage

I try to understand—
read across sources—
across borders, but

every news source I read
is grimmer than the one
I read before.

No. That's wrong. The order
of my reading
doesn't matter—

the spiral of damage
is recursive—reads cumulative
from any direction.

Tonight, I miss my daughter
so hard—she went to live
across the country

in what might be
our last safe year.

Psalm for Day 69
>—*after Psalm 116, verses 15-19*

The sirens sound—
and the dying
are targeting the living
like there was no tomorrow.

I beg YOU
in YOUR sparce rain—
slicken me lose—I want
to be mountain—

a stand-alone forgiveness—
a fat foreclosure
on the unbecoming nature
of revenge—

I want to be breeze
and ligand—transmitter of soft signals
of nurture—eclipsing the damned,
downed telecom.

Maybe I could make YOU
some tea. Do YOU
take honey?
Is there any honey left?

Day 72—Every Deity Will Cry

This virus has completely
taken me out—
I sneeze, I cough, I doze,
I use up my weight
in facial tissues. Rheumy-eyed,
I watch as shifting landscapes
of opinion and anger blur
across my screen. Lachrymose
is such a good word—
teary-eyed, sad.
Our favorite wine is Lacryma Christi
— hard to find in these parts.
But there will be more
of those tears, and soon.

Day 75—I Step Away to Lick Wounds

If a poem
is a tattoo,
I am inked
and scarred
by these
words.

Psalm for Day 76
>—after Psalm 117

Listen! We all
praise differently.

This
is our power—YOUR
love, so big, warm sometimes—YOUR truth

—tessellated, rough-hewn
stones of all colors—sometimes

they don't quite fit
together. The patterns that they make
are unstable, always shifting—and those patterns

are made
from us all.

Day 78, and the news hangs in the air like an overripe fig—

too stubborn to quit
its tree—dripping
it's juice everywhere—

and the juice summons
swarms—and we need them
when they give us honey—

and when they
pollinate us—but
they can also kill—

and they can also
die—and we, we wait—
at their mercy.

Day 80—And I Know Less Every Day

Tomorrow—the full Cold Moon.

The psychological warfare is more than I can etcetera.

Dear friends arrive from Holland.

We pussyfoot for a while, but the truth is this.

Our opinions are riven in the divine expanse,

Testament to past tense.

Witness—speak light.

Come, sit with me for a while.

Come, sit with me.

Day 82—I Want

I am spending money
at our overstocked
market—making a grand dinner
for our guests—and yet
we can't talk
about the war—Israeli
soldiers dying
because "never again"
and they aren't wrong—but
Gazans starving—needing
the basics of life
—like water— I need
a poem driven
by the unbearable
dailyness of this
time—and why can't I ask
"What do you mean"
instead of wedging
my own hot and
sticky and urgent
opinion into it—why
can't you?

Psalm for Day 83
        —after Psalm 118 1-7

I am stilled.
YOUR answers
have silence
between their teeth.

I try to side-eye
YOUR gifts,
not to look at them
head on—superstitious—

for instance,
these friends
come from so far—
the familiar feel

of them—their known-ness—
they gentle me
for a moment—away
from the news cycle,

a guilty pleasure—
the warmth
of my morning shower—
its steam over the mirrors

escalates—then slowly clears.
It gives me hope—
this rhythm—the escalation
followed by de-escalation

every morning—
but then I am
once caught again
in the day's headlines—

steam-blind
and calling out
to YOU in YOUR
divine expanse—

I don't understand
how to find YOU—
at least not reliably—but
I do know how to try.

Come—YOU and I
have work to do—
it feels urgent—
it feels like
an emergency—

but what do I know
of time's cycles?

On Day 84—It's between witchcraft and reading the news

and I choose witchcraft.
How I have missed
spending my evening
casting a circle
setting spells
setting intentions
for all my beloveds—

my candles burning
down to the wick—for my beloved
who is under fire as her
marriage unravels—
the vows she made
holy to her, once
defined her to her core—
her perfect blonde
eyes—her trust
in her God.

For my beloved
who is under fire
in the Ukraine—
her country blanketed
again and again
by the unrelenting
smoke and bombs—I can't
describe the sounds
or the smells
or the fear—or justify
even for a moment
the short-sighted
inadequacy of this country's
reactions.

And one for my beloved whose family
is under fire in Gaza—he hasn't
spoken to me
in a while—how
to reach out?

and this one for the
dear Israeli beloved
under fire in her heart—
pregnant with her first child,
living in New York
while her family
is in Israel, under fire—no mother
near her—

For my beloved who is
under fire in Israel—whose son
is serving in the war—whose
very belief system
is being shattered by the need
to choose one violence
over another—and again
my country, missing the big picture
we are all going to go down with this.
I am just saying.

I've cast all the spells
I have in me tonight.
Tired now, I close
the circle. I write
these words—and then
I read the news
after all.

It's Day 86 and NO

I should probably limit
my alcohol intake
but why? Why

would I want to
prolong this
fortunate life

in the face
of the disasters
that I am not

facing? Shall I not
harp on about
the wars? My child

and how she must
live? This Anthropocene
is fading—

how I love you all.

Psalm for Day 90
    —*after Psalm 118 verses 8-12*

I have a new friend.
She tells me
her truths—they slice
through my own—
they swirl together—
make a kaleidoscope
of truths—all of them
turning unfamiliar—.

No refuge
in common
experience—
all that we have
is this shattered and shared
humanity—
or what's left of it.

We are
surrounded—
enclosed
more than we know—.
We all call
on our gods
as if there were
different ones—.

But what's coming
in this fire of thorns
will take
no sides.

Here's what you need to know 93 days into the war

says one of my news sources.
But no matter how much
I read—I don't 'know' much.

Our daughter is home
from the ICU wars.
She teaches us

that a vasculopath
is someone with
degenerative, inflammatory

functional disorders—
where the blood
can no longer flow.

She thinks of a body—
the internal web of it
in full dysfunction—

killing itself.
Isn't the world
also a body?

Day 95—My Friend Summarizes My Days

You get up
every morning,
dress in blacks
and greys, and
write poetry
about the war.

Day 100 and I Draw Another Line

The moon
in her first quarter—we spend the evening
trying to untangle
feeling from thought from intuition.

I maintain that they are different—
locate differently in the body

But some part of my body
is thinking about the sky—
the light pollution here—
the stars we can't see

the dust and the rubble there
where so many children sleep—
each part of their bodies
hungry—

Day 104: Can YOU Open Me Up
—after Psalm 118 versus 19-24

for I have been
closed and in the dark
for 104 days—

guide me towards
the white stones
of YOUR city—the particular

pearl-glow of them—
YOUR generosity,
which I tend to forget

in the singe and burn
of these days—but there
they are—YOUR gates—

Day 107 of War in the Holy Lands: Heart Wants

I'm telling myself it's OK to start a new notebook—nothing magic about it.

Heart goes 'NO! New notebook = magic (for sure)—means a whole new notebook of war—gotta wait—gotta wait for peace.'

But truth about it is that my notebook is full—and I've regressed to envelopes, mailer scraps, receipts—i.e. chaos—matching outfits—me & the world—twins in gaudy dresses. Not a great look.

Heart wants music—wants Wagner's four minutes of E flat major—epic—(damn antisemite)—genius musician—heart wants, heart wants the wood and linen of the fine concert hall heart wants space for all the people—heart wants to make heart-deals across acrimony—heart wants everyone to be powerless so that they know…

Heart wants a new notebook.

Day 110? 111? I Looked Away for a Moment

and those men—
the ones mad
with power—
made drear decisions

and their souls
are forfeit
—and by proxy—
ours

Day 118—The Proper Way to Phrase a Prayer for Peace
—after Psalm 118 verses 25-29

What if I ask
for the wrong thing?
My words are imprecise,
and YOU tend
towards the literal.

I'm listening to the noise
that the hours make—waiting
for my heart
to soften—waiting
for the ribbons
that bind me
to loosen—

    and then
I might know
what to ask—and how
to ask for it.

Postlude

—IT ISN'T OVER—

Swarm
        —after Psalm 119 verses 1-2

My heart risks it all—says
generous—but my mind
is wily, unkind—these war days
drag me down—seaweed
in precarious seas—

disoriented—the sea's floor
lost to me for holdfast—no latch & tug
can't drag myself up to the shoreline—
salty & dripping & sure
that this time

that I've found YOUR way
—as if it were
up for interpretation—

but I do, YOU know—
I interpret furiously—

and now, scraping down
through the fury—cruelty
—at the bottom
of it all, at the lowest
point—my ears
hear YOUR whisper:

the whole heart
will find me—

Leap Day
   —after Psalm 119 verses 1-4

To walk happy—painless—tireless—I want to say that I dream it—but it's more like a waking dream—I lose my way in the morning kitchen—put coffee grinds in the coffee cup and sugar in the coffee pot—dreaming of pathways through the day—

news silenced for once—the heart wants to open—the heart wants to find YOU again—the heart and her rampant desires—

the heart wants to get the taste of dust out of her mouth—she wants silence and the perfect music together and at once—I give her permission to look away just for this one imaginary day in our strange calendars—

a day of floating—a messy blessing—a day of surrender—lost again in YOUR inscrutable
user's manual.

Sin-Mouths
    —after Psalm 59

This is the work of our own blood—

 recovery

   reaching back

to before—
as if YOU would give us
what we think we need

   which is always
   yesterday—
   which is redo, repeat.

Take them—these lies of repair—

   —dripping
   as if from rabid
   dogmaws—

   Argus impersonators

    —and they are hungry

  hellhounds— not
     to be trusted

    —waiting for us
    to finish
    our destructions

  and then—they
    will finish
    their own

Locksmith
        —after Psalm 110

I made the key—I made
the frozen lock—and when I can manage
YOUR presence, YOU
disappear them—they are, after all,
only constructs.

Imagine
God's mind—YOUR mind
which has made me

into a holy being—sometimes
I am generous
—sometimes
I shatter on the coastlines
of a conversation

—or break
at our loss
of decency—

until YOU lift
my face
again—the long trek back
towards kindness
—and I begin

Warm Evening, Restless
    — after Psalm 104 lines 25-30

    The sea, being

moonstruck   a playground   a cloud reading—a card drawn in reverse
—a moist body   it holds   its breath   as if for solstice—hungry

for YOUR grace.   I imagine the sea—foraging   in its damp
spirit   for signs   signals of YOUR   arrival

    —when YOU provide   —let me be   the sea
      (she who is always watched & thus always watchful— she sloshes
        she who has   seen   the signs)

    —when YOU open YOUR hand   —let me be   the sea
      (she who is   immense   she who is   always
        ready   to receive)

& when YOU turn   away   —and YOU *will*   turn away
—again— let me be   gracious   let me relinquish   my breath, my bones—

dissolve   into altar   —into footstool and wing   until YOU
breathe out   —again—   over   the land

—Imagine   being restored   in the season
of YOUR breath

Crow Comes Back
—after Psalm 104 verses 20-24

YOU and I, we have cycled through days and years and seasons I can't name, and I don't know what pulls us together, or what pulls us apart. The sun rises, the sun sets, and one day I will lie with YOU, and I am not ready. Selah.

Blessed is the darkness—how I need it. I light the candles to entice my animals to emerge, and sometimes—shy, camouflaged, feathered, crowned in ferns and thistles, flammable, bright eyed, wily, they come. Sometimes they nuzzle. Sometimes nip.

I still have work to do. And I want to talk about the moon, but I'll admit, I am no good at writing about her cycles—we are too close—her light, my darkness—and really, all of it

is YOURS.

In darkness, I reach out, which is not to say that I don't reach out in daylight, but isn't it the dimming of the days that lengthens our reach? Isn't it the blurring that brings, finally, focus?

NOTES

The hashtag epigraph for *Day 4 of the War* (page 9) by Dana Levin is from her poem *Heroic Couplet* from her book *Now Do You Know Where You Are,*

The borrowed line from Adélia Prado in *Day 4 of the War* (page 9) is from her poem *Dysrhythmia* from her book *The Alphabet in the Park*

The two poems referred to in *Love Poem for Day 39* (page 20) are Ada Limon's poem *The End of Poetry* from her book *The Hurting Kind* and Aracelis Girmay's poem *"You are Who I Love"* from Belladonna chaplet #229 *Mother Mother You are Who I Love*

The poet referred to in *Psalm for Day 42 of the War* (page 21) is the Yiddish Poet Aaron Glants Leyeles in his poem *The God of Israel.*

The Wagner piece referred to in *Day 107 of War in the Holy Lands: Heart Wants* (page 44) is *"Das Rheingold"* Prelude.

ACKNOWLEDGMENTS

With thanks to the editors of the journals who published poems from this collection:

American Academy of Poets
　　Hoof

Gashmius Magazine
　　Fragment for Day 20 of the Israel-Hamas War—after Psalm 116 verses 1-4
　　On Day 34 of the Israel-Hamas War I Ask YOU to Teach Us Again —after Psalm 116
　　Psalm for Day 42 of the Israel-Hamas War —after Psalm 116 verses 9-14

Minyan Magazine
　　Day 4 of the Israel-Hamas War,
　　On Day 17 of the Israel-Hamas War—She Asks Me,

Volume
　　Psalm for day 83
　　A Prayer for the Ability to Pray

Janus Head: Journal of Interdisciplinary Studies in Literature, Continental Philosophy, Phenomenological Psychology, and the Arts
　　Backbone
　　Warm Evening, Restless

Alaska Poetry Review (Volume 40 No. 3 & 4, Summer & Fall 2024)
　　Crow Comes Back

Pensive
　　The Proper Way to Phrase a Prayer for Peace

So much gratitude goes to my poets Nan Cohen and Laura Hogan, who have been with me for years, who read most of these poems, and who encouraged me to continue in what I was sure was madness.

Gratitude also to my poets Suzanne Edison and Heidi Seaborne, for picking up towards the end of this journey and helping me titrate the most stubborn of these poems.

Thank you, Laura Reece Hogan, for bringing Wildhouse Poetry and this book together, and thank you Wildhouse and Mark S. Burrows for seeing these poems, and for giving them a home. Thank you to the team at Wildhouse, Ava O'Malley for your tireless support behind the scenes, and Melody Stanford Martin, who made this beautiful cover for me. It is stunning. It is perfect.

For the essential warmth of the community that you continue to provide for me, even in cold and dark times, thank you Roy White, Meghan Dunn, Allison Albino, Christian Collier, Julia Kolchinsky, Carly DeMento, Flower Conroy, and all my loves at Yetzirah, A Hearth for Jewish Poetry. And thank you, my daughter, Mishala Bateman, you are wise beyond your years.

To my Psalms Sisters, Debra Linesch, Anne Brenner, Thelma Samulon, Davia Rivka, and Darcy Vebber, thank you for the years of study and writing and discussion and friendship.

During all the years of Lectio Divina study of the psalms, I wearied of all our names for the holy, the universe, the deity, the G-d or G-dess, however you refer to the all-encompassing wonder. Every name holds only one aspect of the holy up to the light, and almost every name is gendered. Also, the third person-ness of the names began to feel distant. I wanted dialogue, argument, closeness. The 'You' that people often use didn't seem big enough, and somehow, I came to think of the all-encompassing as YOU. I am grateful for this journey to YOU.

Finally, to Gershom Spruijt—my love—you were here to talk all these thoughts and feelings and ideas through with me—to imagine this collection—but you never got to see the book. Thank you for all the years, for the 'great relief of having you to talk to.' Your stunning tree drawings are hidden here and there throughout the collection. You were my shelter, and I miss you deeply.
Let there be light. Let there be love. Let there be peace.

ABOUT THE AUTHOR

Donna Spruijt-Metz is an emeritus professor of psychology, MacDowell fellow, rabbinical school drop-out, and former classical flutist. Featured as one of "5 over 50 debut authors" in *Poets & Writers Magazine* (January, 2023), her chapbooks include *Slippery Surfaces*, And *Haunt the World* (with Flower Conroy), and Dear Ghost, winner of the 2023 Harbor Review Editor's prize. She lived in the Netherlands for twenty-two years and translates Dutch poetry. Her poems and translations appear at the Academy of American Poets and, most recently, in the *Tahoma Literary Review*, *Alaska Quarterly Review*, *Copper Nickel*, and *The American Poetry Review* ((forthcoming). Her collaborative book with Flower Conroy, And *Scuttle My Balloon*, is forthcoming (Pictureshow Press, 2025) as is her translation from the Dutch of Lucas Hirsch's *Wu Wei Eats an Egg* (Ben Yehuda Press, 2025). Learn more at www.donnasmetz.com.

ABOUT THE ARTIST

Gershom Spruijt was born in the Netherlands and lived for many years in Amsterdam. From his years observing the old Amsterdam canals and visiting the fine Dutch art from the Golden Age, he developed the idea that the 1960's were perhaps not superior to the 1690s. After getting his PhD in Psychology and Epidemiology at the University of Amsterdam, he moved to Los Angeles to study sculpture and later painting at Otis College of Art and Design. At the Art Center College of Design, he taught classes on imagination and on the neuropsychology of perception. He also taught drawing and composition and rendering in oil paint. He lectured locally and internationally on perception and imagination and lived happily with his wife, daughter and two dogs in Los Angeles. His Dutch name, Robertus Spruijt, is hard to pronounce for English speakers, so he always signed his work with his Hebrew name, Gershom.

This book is set in *Optima* typeface, developed by the German type- designer and calligrapher Hermann Zapf. Its inspiration came during Zapf's first trip to Italy in 1950. While in Florence he visited the cemetery of the Basilica di Santa Croce and was immediately taken by the design of the lettering found on the old tombstones there. He quickly sketched an early draft of the design on a 1000 lire banknote, and after returning to Frankfurt devoted him- self to its development. It was first released as Optima by the D. Stempel AG foundry in 1958 and shortly thereafter by Mergenthaler in the United States. Inspired by classical Roman inscriptions and distinguished by its flared terminals, this typeface is prized for its curves and straights which vary minutely in thickness, providing a graceful and clear impression to the eye.